Hazards of Eden

Hazards of Eden:

Poems from the Southwest

Glen Sorestad

Copyright © 2015 Glen Sorestad
All Rights Reserved

ISBN: 978-1-942956-03-7
Library of Congress Control Number: 2015938246

Lamar University Press
Beaumont, Texas

Acknowledgments

In gathering together these poems of the Southwest, I have included several poems that first appeared in three of my earlier books of poems: *Air Canada Owls* (1984), *Blood & Bone, Ice & Stone* (2005) and *Road Apples* (2009). Some of those poems have undergone changes since their original publication. I am grateful to Harbour Publishing, Thistledown Press and Rubicon Press for publishing those respective volumes.

Other poems appeared in earlier versions and sometimes with different titles in the following literary publications and the author is grateful to their editors:
Poetry Monthly International
The Mesquite Review
Nose Mountain Moods
Texas Poetry Calendar
Kaleidoscope Journal

Poetry from Lamar University Press

Alan Berecka, *With Our Baggage*
David Bowles, *Flower, Song, Dance*: Aztec *and Mayan Poetry* (a new translation)
Jerry Bradley, *Crownfeathers and Effigies*
Chip Dameron, *Waiting for an Etcher*
William Virgil Davis, *The Bones Poems*
Jeffrey DeLotto, *Voices Writ in Sand*
Mimi Ferebee, *Wildfires and Atmospheric Memories*
Ken Hada, *Margaritas and Redfish*
Michelle Hartman, *Disenchanted and Disgruntled*
Katherine Hoerth, *Goddess Wears Cowboy Boots*
Lynn Hoggard, *Motherland*
Gretchen Johnson, *A Trip Through Downer, Minnesota*
Janet McCann, *The Crone at the Casino*
Erin Murphy, *Ancilla*
Dave Oliphant, *The Pilgrimage, Selected Poems: 1962-2012*
Kornelijus Platelis, *Solitary Architectures,* translated by Jonas Zdanys
Carol Coffee Reposa, *Underground Mucicians*
Jan Seale, *The Parkinson Poems*
Carol Smallwood, *Water, Earth, Air, Fire, and Picket Fences*

For information on these and other Lamar University Press books go to
www.LamarUniversityPress.Org

For
the memory of the poet Keith Wilson
the teacher and raconteur Henry Devilliers
the teacher poet/playwright Tony Clark
all three true sons of the Southwest
from whom I have learned to love the land
within which they are at rest

CONTENTS

xi   Preface

I. Drive Friendly

15   Hazards of Eden
16   A Brush with Religion
17   Welcome to Galveston
18   The Texan from Romania
19   Fishing Report from the Seawall
21   Winter in Galveston
22   Galveston, 2003
24   Life is a Highway
25   Hard Scrabble Clouds
26   The Viet Nam Vet Reads in Brownsville
28   Hunting Farms
29   Sleeping in Amarillo
30   The Grackle Joined us for Lunch
32   The Big Texan Steak Ranch
33   Veterans' Day in Brownsville
35   Fisherman on South Padre Island
36   Cowboy Christ

II. Desert Musings

39   Chihuahuan Desert
40   Big Bend Suite
41   Desert Tarantula
42   Dangerous Places
43   Running on Taurus Mesa
44   Desert Reflections

III. Llano Estacado

47	Gila Wilderness Chili
48	Missiles for Artesia
49	Llano Estacado
51	Lake Maloya
52	Last Meeting in Las Cruces
55	November Hawks
56	Being Cast in Gallup
57	Mesa-top Lakes
58	The Backyard World of Joe Somoza
59	Pinons and Pine Nuts
60	If Place Names Mean Anything
61	After the Fall
62	After the Poetry Reading in New Mexico
63	Two Old Boys in a Half-ton
65	UNM Crows
67	The Dancing Man of Santa Elena
68	Fifty Thousand Coyotes Can't Be Wrong
70	Sea Dreams/War Dreams
71	Incident in Las Cruces
72	Satisfaction Required

IV. There Were Signs

75	Trouble in La Junta
76	Whatever Happened to Jane Jayroe?
78	Easy Proof
79	Mesa Verde
80	Narrow Gauge Railroad, Colorado
82	Main Street in Scottsdale
83	They Said
86	There Were Signs

V. Road Apples (excerpts)

Preface

I believe it was in 1981 that I made my first trip down into the part of America that is commonly spoken of as the Southwest. A few years earlier, I had met Keith Wilson, one of New Mexico's splendidly gifted poets, at a writing conference called "Crossing Frontiers" in Banff in the Canadian Rockies. I was intensely attracted to the poems that he presented during the conference because I sensed that what he wrote about New Mexico's landscape and people was what I felt and what I wanted to express about my own place and people. When I was invited by Keith to come down to New Mexico to give a reading, it didn't take me long to decide to go—and thus began my long and continuing fascination with the Southwest, call it a love affair if you wish, and one I'm happy to say is still flourishing.

Since that first trip I have lost count of the number of times I have now visited New Mexico and Texas especially, but also parts of Oklahoma, Arizona, Colorado, Nevada and Utah. But my fascination has focused mainly on New Mexico and Texas and in later years on parts of the Chihuahuan Desert, notably in that area of western Texas known as the Big Bend country.

When I travel anywhere, I write poems. That is just how it is with me. It's what I do and it's how I respond to things that capture my attention, that stimulate my interest and that pique my curiosity. I can no more avoid writing poems during my travels than I can avoid breathing. It's just who I am. I don't pretend to be anything more than an interested observer as I move through the Southwest. My impressions are certainly no more or less valid than any other traveller moving through the same space at the same time. I am certainly an outsider, unaware of a great many things and seeing through an occasional visitor's eyes, not with the eyes of one who has lived there for a long time. In that sense, many of the poems may present the familiar, but through eyes that lack the knowledge and expectations of one who is a native to the land. Sometimes that is not such a bad thing. Sometimes we need to see ourselves and our surroundings through the eyes of a newcomer. It may surprise us to realize that there are often unusual ways of seeing the familiar. Good poems will often do that for a reader.

While these are poems that have their origins in those parts of the Southwest that I have seen firsthand and experienced in some small part, they are as much about me as they are about this strangely beautiful land that draws me back to it again and again. The poems are the written manifestations of what has captured and held my attention, even for a moment, of things that have impressed themselves upon me. So I cannot claim that they are anything more than one Canadian writer's take on those moments and experiences that have helped to shape not only what he has written, but indeed the writer himself.

From my first introduction to the Southwest by Keith Wilson, I have been blessed, over the considerable number of intervening years, to have been welcomed into the warmth and generous hospitality of the homes and friendships of so many wonderful people in New Mexico and Texas. Some of the poems pay tribute to a few of these people, but to all of those generous folks who have welcomed this traveller into their lives, I am eternally grateful and these poems are a way of saying how pleased I have been to be among you.

Glen Sorestad, January 2015

I. Drive Friendly

Hazards of Eden

We walk tentative, careful steps—shorter, more deliberate than usual.
The day is warm, humid. We scrutinize the path ahead, eyes alert

to the fringe of the walkway. We oohed and aahed the orchid house,
the bromeliad house, and a dazzling array of tropical plants sustained

by weather and human care at South Texas Botanical Gardens. Now,
we are away from the cloistered plants, we are warned that there are

snakes, venomous ones, as part of the Gardens' offering, though we
had not counted on viewing such at all. We are advised that should we

encounter a Diamondback Rattlesnake, or other such unfriendly serpent
on the trail, we should *back off, slowly*—advice I consider redundant,

though the *slowly* part strikes me as a non-starter. After dazzling dozens
of orchids and a booty of bromeliads, our unfettered pleasure

in the floral offerings has been sullied by serpentine warnings,
to such a degree that my ears strain to detect the least rattle or buzz,

or a papery slither in the undergrowth, my eyes imagining coils, signs
of the "narrow fellow in the grass." There is always a snake in the Garden.

A Brush with Religion

South of San Antonio on I-37 as we drive towards Corpus Christi
we are startled by a sign: *Brush Country Cowboy Church*.
I look around. Brush land—no question. The car purrs, my head hums.

Behind the wheel I am imagining leathery cowboys astride cow ponies,
lean and craggy-faced riders, well-weathered, looking suspiciously
like the Duke or even Randolph Scott, butting their horses through

rough tangles of scrub growth. I hear saddles creak, horses snort,
as they rein their mounts to this deserty place of worship to pray
for beef prices to surge to new highs and stay there; to pray for

a Republican President who will protect and preserve with vigilance
the sanctity of private ownership and the right of god-fearing ranchers
to reign supreme—lords of black Angus herds and white Escalades.

Welcome to Galveston

a found poem

JUST US AND GUNS!

Concealed Handgun Classes

Beginners Welcome!

6 HOUR CLASSES

Monday – Sunday

classified ad in the *Galveston Daily News*, December 27, 2013

The Texan from Romania

Lunch in Landry's in Galveston and the winter sun,
in hiding for days, has burst apart the grey to splash
across the shifting Gulf, to glitter the sandscape,
and evoke a smile from every face.

The young woman who serves us says her name
is Aline. Her name-plate says *Alina,* and as she gives us
our menus I note a Slavic inflection, not all her words,
just certain ones come out decidedly un-Texan-like,
so I say to her, "You're not Texan, Aline, are you?"
She shakes her head.

"So where are you from?" Alina is from Romania,
lived in Houston five years, moved to Galveston
just three months ago. My curiosity is piqued.
But as much as I'd like to probe deeper,
a voice inside is saying,
You don't really want to go there,
a voice imbued with dark memories of films,
news reports, stories and articles about
how so many young women from Eastern Europe
were victimized and ended up in America.
I doubt Alina arrived as one of the unfortunates,
but I do not intend to darken the joy
of a day like today—for either of us.

Fishing Report from the Seawall

*You see where that man is fishin',
right down there by that big rock?
Well, I caught ten redfish there,
one day last week, and four flounder,
a couple of trout, too,* she says.
Wanna see what they looked like?

She is sitting in her Chevy half-ton,
parked alongside our rental Equinox,
window rolled down, waving her I-phone
to show us her fish photos. Proof.
She's Afro-American, Galveston-born,
maybe a decade younger than we are,
lives in an apartment off the Seawall,
and right now she wants an audience.
We are total strangers who might fill
a little slow time in her day,
talk with her, even listen a while.
We ooh and aah over her fish images.

Did you use shrimp for bait? I ask.

*Yeah, I did. I was going home from work
and I smelled this fish-bait in the back,
must have been getting old because
it sure was smelly, so I figure I gotta
use it or lose it and I came here.
And I was fishin' right down there
where that guy is sittin' right now,
though he ain't caught nothing yet.*
She flashes a satisfied grin.

Guess those fish liked smelly shrimp,
didn't they? I say. She nods, still brandishing
her I-phone, as if the entire experience
defied any reasonable explanation,
as if by uttering it and presenting her I-proof,
the wonder of it might become evident.

Did you eat all that fish? I ask.
No, it's almost all in my freezer.
I live alone, you know. You can only
eat fish so many times a week.

When we back our vehicle away,
I notice the I-phone woman has
wasted little time attracting to her truck
a younger woman; by the way she
flourishes her I-phone, I know she
has yet another fish on the line.

Winter in Galveston

The Yellow Cab mini-van
picks us up at our hotel to deliver us
to Gaido's Seafood Restaurant,
further down the Seawall.
An affable Haitian named Jean
is our driver. He has a woman
riding in the front seat as co-pilot.
We crawl into the back.

Enroute Jean tells us he's now
ten years removed from the poverty
and never-ending strife of his island homeland.
When we tell him about the cold
we have left, he shakes his head
in near-disbelief, as if the mere thought
of temperatures in negative digits
is data a Haitian imagination
cannot fathom. He wears a down-filled jacket
because it is cold. It is sixty degrees F,
warm enough for us. Weather and chance
have brought all of us together,
a convergence of strangers,
all of us drawn here to weather
our time in this place.

Galveston, 2003

It is the very same sea.
From one century to the next
the waters of the Gulf press
a wet hand on Galveston sand,
just as they did last year,
last century, just as they did
that day over a hundred years ago
when Isaac Cline refused
to accept the signs,
refuted the possibility
of a monster storm that would
end up taking the lives
of much of his own family
and six thousand more
on Galveston Island.

It is this very same sea,
ceaseless in its movement,
today, innocuous
as a well behaved pet.
But in 1900, driven
to unimagined fury
and unspeakable violence,
it swamped a city's dream.

I look at the rolling waves
from the balcony of a condo
where countless thousands
before me have sat
and gazed at this restless
give and take
of the great tumbling sea

and I wonder how many
tried to imagine that day
when Galveston drowned,
only to be resurrected,
seventeen feet higher than before,
beyond the expected reaches
of that mostly good-natured sea
tossing its watery syllables
to scatter across the pages of sand?

Life is a Highway

We drive the interstate towards San Antonio,
and I am enjoying being behind the wheel
of this rented German road machine that clings
to the road and purrs contentedly to itself.

A sign announces the next exit as COMFORT.
I pass without comment, but I do note
how appropriate it feels, here, this moment.
Inside the Passat all is well. Comfort indeed.

Further along the concrete another sign says
the next exit, believe it or not, WELFARE.
Only in Texas, can one forsake Comfort
for Welfare and still be on the right road.

Hard Scrabble Clouds

Beneath this unmarred blue
the only clouds today

lie just above the russet soil
on stems of ripening cotton.

The Viet Nam Vet Reads in Brownsville

There are soldiers in airports,
all in sand-coloured camouflage.
They may be arriving,
or perhaps awaiting flights,
the latest recruits
for the never-ending wars.

This is the image that grabs us:
soldiers in airports,
waiting—forever bound
either to or from
ever-shifting fields of slaughter.

The reader, who has been there
and who has returned,
has waited out his hours
dressed in sand drab
or jungle green, has seen
the worst things man can
and does do to his own kind.

The agony of each take-off,
each landing, are fangs,
the venom destroying
what we call soul or spirit.
His are the words
of the faceless warrior,
awaiting his own deliverance
or his own demise,
devoid of feeling.

We bleed with every word
he rips from the pages
of his book of pain.

Hunting Farms

In the vast rolling ranch country
south of San Angelo sprawl 100,000 acres
owned by the Sugg family.
As you skirt the high wire fences
along Route 163, a sign on one gate
announces *Bar None Hunt Company*,
how decidedly ironic,
since hunting on the ranch
is restricted to those with deep pockets
or deeper connections. Anyone else
need not inquire. The property is
secure as a prison.

Hunt is also an ironic word.
You see blinds or raised shooting stands
at various locations, around which feed
is scattered to lure deer or turkeys
or wild boar within shooting range,
so that the *hunters*
do not have to actually walk,
or to stalk their prey,
as the word *hunt* implies.
They can sit in comfort
and wait for animals to come.

Sleeping in Amarillo

Last night in our RV
we slept ten solid hours—
something my insomniac friend
would find inconceivable.

While locked in our tower
of dreams, constant interstate
tire whine drove the commerce
of America, oblivious to us.

Boxcars of freight punctuated
the dark on clacking rails,
with wails of locomotives
an industrial nocturne.

A Grackle Joined Us for Lunch
for Chip Dameron

I don't think any of us invited the bird.

Grackles do not rate high on most lists
of desirable luncheon companions,
but it showed up nonetheless,
like an old friend you'd almost forgotten.
It perched on the back of a chair
at a nearby table like someone's
left-behind hat, looked around,
as if expecting its significant other
to make a tardy appearance.

To fill time it broke out in song
and in rapid order flipped from one
startling outburst to another in its repertoire,
as if practising, perhaps,
or beckoning us to choose—
pick a song, any song—
switching tunes like a teen
on the family car radio dial.

Having exhausted its selection,
the grackle cocked an expectant eye,
trying to gauge how impressed we were:
Isn't that worthy of an invitation?

We did our best to ignore the bird,
while it did all it could to entertain.
I perceived a slight sag in its demeanor,
a touch of relenting
in its saucy impudence,
watched its feathers unpuff
with a hint of having failed,
that is, until it spotted new arrivals
who might prove to be far more
susceptible to being regaled
by an avian impressionist
and off it flew to perch at another table,
eyeing a new audience like a sorcerer
sizing up volunteers for the next trick.

The Big Texan Steak Ranch

At a time when more than half the children
in the world are undernourished,
many dying or debilitated for lack of food,
it would seem a gross indecency,
an insult to the famished,
to find a restaurant that encourages diners
to commit the sin of sheer gluttony
by eating, or trying to eat seventy-two ounces
of beef steak, along with all the extras,
FREE
if you can devour the gargantuan meal,
trimmings and all, *entirely*,
and do so within one hour.

Most nutritionists, let alone
anyone with a lick of common sense
would be adamant that four and a half
pounds of beef in a single meal constitutes
what should be an indictable offense.

Yet here in Amarillo
we are urged to poison ourselves
with a cholesterol tsunami
enough to destroy a normal digestive system,
not to mention clog a thousand miles of arteries
and keep heart and stroke specialists
gainfully busy, all in the name of keeping
ranchers raising their prize herds of black Angus.

In the land of excess we just close our eyes,
slap the faces of the impoverished
and pretend we deserve what we have.

Veterans' Day in Brownsville

Home, where we call this *Remembrance Day*,
lies almost a hundred degrees Fahrenheit north.
On both sides of the border we take a day
in November to honor those who've been
asked to give too much. We give kids
a school day off and silently pray we'll never
have to ask our own children to have to kill.

On Veterans' Day in Brownsville,
I think of the uncle I never met, killed
on Juno Beach in a war become more distant
with each generation; I think of my poet-friend
in Las Cruces, his hearing destroyed
by the shelling of Korean shoreline;
I think of another who went to Viet Nam
and others who refused to go,
their lives forever shaken, either way.

On Veterans' Day in Brownsville
I think of young women and men in Iraq
and in Afghanistan—all the vets-to-be
and the ones who'll return in body bags,
what's left of them consigned to rest
within the regimented precision of a dazzle
of white marble crosses, constant reminder
of the horrific cost of our beliefs
and the price we pay for failed leaders.

On Veterans' Day in Brownsville
I think of all those like me, born too early
or too late, those spared from having
to ship out to distant death, spared from

bearing the dolorous weight of warfare,
spared the equal burden a state places
on each generation it recruits
and trains to kill or be killed.

On Veterans' Day in Brownsville
I am thankful for my naivety,
thankful I've been spared the unspeakable,
thankful to dream each night
with no horrors of trench or jungle brutality,
no mustard gas or agent orange
or incendiary nightmares.

Today I remember my fallen uncle,
my poet-friends, lives indelibly altered,
those who returned and those who didn't.
On this day in south Texas I remember
all of these and I sing for them.

Fisherman on South Padre Island

He has exchanged frozen lakes
for miles of sand and restless Gulf.
Most mornings he rises early, alone
to this stretch of beach to fish,
his only company the crash of surf.

He parks his half-ton, pulls on waders,
gears himself to stand in the swell
and ebb of booming sea. He casts
his fresh, shrimp-baited hook
out to the gathering waves,

as far as his weighted line will go.
To fish the Gulf is history, time itself—
shrimped hook, predatory fish,
temptation, instinct. Rod in holder,
jammed in sand, 25 pound test line

taut, rod aquiver like a nervous filly
at the starting gate, the fisherman
from Kentucky or Vermont, Wisconsin
or Minnesota stands alert. He waits,
eyes on the line, the tension.

The sun on his face is warm. Gulls
wheel and dip above the waves.
He cannot imagine being anywhere
other than here, today, in this place.
The blue Gulf advances and recedes.

Cowboy Christ
remembering Tony Clark

In Paris, Texas Christ rises above
the final rest of Willet Babcock,
the long-dead rancher well anchored
for fierce winds. Babcock cares little

for the three of us, drawn here
not for prayers over his bones,
but to stare, as we do now, up
at this sculpted Christ astride

Babcock's massive headstone
that derricks twenty feet against
a wintry Texas sky, His shoulder
against the cross, flowing robe

to his feet. We are poets all, two
fled south from a frozen land
to follow our Texas colleague here
to scuff the stony path to Babcock,

though the pebbles we dislodge above
are bootless to his ears as we assume
the perfect vantage point to see
beneath the robe of Jesus His left foot,

His cowboy boot. Why shouldn't I believe
in Texas even He would wear boots?
For the moment we are silent here,
gathered around the feet of Christ.

II. Desert Musings

Chihuahuan Desert

Unforgiving terrain
where the right footwear
trumps the right shirt;
where proper headwear
is a proper attitude;
where spikes and spines
vie with thorns and burrs;
where a straight line
is seldom the shortest
distance between points;
where water, not oil,
is liquid currency.

Go to the desert alone
and you had better know
all these things
and much more besides.
You can survive
an occasional mistake,
a time or two perhaps.
It will be the small,
seemingly insignificant
lapse of judgment
that will exact
the harshest penalty.

Big Bend Suite

   1.

Chihuahuan desert:
spring is a horseman fording
the Rio heading north.

   2.

The mountain lion
turns darkness into danger
high in the Chisos.

   3.

Santa Elena:
canyon carved by Rio Grande
to sheer sandstone walls.

   4.

From desert roadsides
cheering us with spring's promise:
Big Bend bluebonnets.

   5.

Spring sun awakens
slumbering yucca cacti—
flowerbursts of snow.

Desert Tarantula

The creature inched its eight-legged way
across the yard, the largest spider I've seen—

one that would dwarf a child's hand—
its design and colouration, furred and striking,

one any entomologist could truly love,
a dangerous beauty, or so it appeared to us

northerners, as out of place in its New Mexico
world as it would be in ours. I called a local

to identify for me this unfamiliar creeper.
One brief glance and: *It's not a good thing*,

she said before stomping the heel of her shoe
with absolute judgment on the tarantula.

Dangerous Places

A desert can be an inhospitable landscape—needles and spines,
stingers and fangs hiding their malice at every turn.
Every rock ledge, every depression can conceal a potential attack,
diamondback coils in wait of the unwary foot.

A desert campfire, four men talk, the topic loops around to snakes:

*I've been here twelve years now and I've only seen three rattlers
in all that time,* says one.

*I've been camping here eight years
and I'm still looking for my first,*
says another.

*I've lived in New Mexico twenty-five years
and I've encountered just one rattlesnake,* says the third.
*It wasn't in the desert either, but when I lived in town.
Came right up on my back deck
and I hadda get my gun and kill it,*
says the third.

The fourth says nothing. He is thinking
about the desert. He thinks it is a place
of dangerous misconceptions.

Running on Taurus Mesa

A man is running across the desert.
It is early morning, but already the sun
rides the rim of the Chisos Mountains.
A light breeze cools him as he runs.
He does not flee from danger,
nor from his own actions or failures;
nor to some distant expectation.

The man loves to run, loves the morning,
loves this Chihuahuan desert mesa
where he is the only palpable movement
in an otherwise static scene,
so far as any camera eye can see.

The man is conscious of none of this
as he runs, careful of where his feet
fall, where small dangers lie, where
loose stones or rocks can wrench
an ankle, bruise sole or heel.
Yet some part of him feels
he moves across an action screen
to a script of his own writing,
knows this each time he runs
here on Taurus Mesa. Other nights when
he is home asleep, many miles from here,
he dreams running past yucca and mesquite,
intent on a goal that always eludes him.

Desert Reflections

While I am drawn to it
and desire it take me in,
I am not sure it can or will.
It recognizes a stranger.

Something in me is
wary, on constant alert,
suspicious of the velvet
softness of its colours—

I know the hardness
of stone lies below.
This land is not mine,
nor am I sure it can be.

Even a coyote nocturne
cannot make me feel
fully at home—
something it cannot be.

III. Llano Estacado

Gila Wilderness Chili
for Jim Harris

I am stirring a large pot of chili—ground beef, a Spanish onion,
a large can of Mexican tomatoes, another of jalapeno pinto beans,

simmering on a Coleman camp stove. Gusts of zesty spices fill me
with intense well being—nothing here unusual, except that I am

standing before this camp stove set atop a cement-embedded
campground table close by the cliff dwellings in the Gila Wilderness

in New Mexico and there's not a soul around as I stir the chili, no one
I can see at all this winter evening as darkness drops, the place empty

but for me and the zingy bursts of chili spices wafting up the slopes,
rising into the overhead cliff dwellings and drifting down the Gila River.

I am alone in fading light as I stand here and stir, alone with my chili
in a place that would at other times be loud with visitors, alone, but for

deer who come to the Gila River to drink, then lurk, silent on the fringe
of the campground, curious about the two-legs who must be the source

of the disgusting smell that infests the area, perhaps intruding on dreams
of hibernators, perhaps stirring spirits of the ancient Mogollan, who

peopled the overhead cliffs centuries ago and who just may have looked
down on my slow stirring with kindness. I think all these things as I

stir the concoction, keep the chili from burning, let the flavours blend;
I think I may also be cooking up a poem—about Gila Wilderness chili

and neither I nor anyone else will ever be able to duplicate this moment:
not the chili, nor the feeling. I listen, wait, as the darkness enfolds me.

Missiles for Artesia
for Peter Christensen

Our rented Aries packed with poems we roll
      over the White Sand Missile Range. A blockade
           of the US Army mars our journey's cadence.
The young MP in dappled khaki, black boots
      agleam like a sun-polished Raven, announces
           we have to sit here for an hour and wait:
the missiles of language and love we bear
      from Canada to the waiting few in Artesia
           are stalemated by American LC 50s.
But even the flash and smoke and streak
      of portents from the Pentagon will not
           deter us—only keen the edge of our intent.
We are allowed to resume our mission.
      In Artesia the people wait. We lob our poems
           down from the Sacramento Mountains.

                New Mexico, March 1987

Llano Estacado

Staked plains. Texas cattle range climbs
west to the caprock, gives way to *llano estacado,*
cotton farms and oilfields, staked today
with fences and steel donkeys, nodding,
drawing crude from the depths.

Centuries ago conquistadors rode
Spanish horses across this land, staked
claim to the treeless plain, staked their
agarophobic way, left their markers
and staked the heart of the Southwest
for Spain, lost it finally at the Alamo.

The wind runs unhindered, runs east
from the mountains of New Mexico
across the rough roll of longhorn Texas,
while we speed west, climb the caprock
west onto fields of cotton and peanuts.
We know nothing of parched Spaniards
riding the fire of desert summer
four hundred years before us, awed
and fearful as their water dwindled.

We roll over the *llano estacado,* nothing
at stake, ignorant of the past, drinking
cold Coronas as we go, unconcerned
about any shortage of watering holes.
We roll west through Texas towns
clinging precariously to hardscrabble soil
in wind from New Mexico that would

unstake them and spin them east.
Llano estacado lies ahead like a sea.
We skim the waves, leave no wake.
The wind pays us no heed.

Lake Maloya

At the moment of that first
abrupt jolt to the monofilament
spun out onto the water,

that signal an eager rainbow trout
had smacked my spinning lure,
the tiny lake nestled above the oaks

of Sugarite Canyon in northern
New Mexico was reeled from myth
to flop on the banks of reality.

Five trout later it was fact,
to be retold and later embellished,
recast in its new mythic shape.

Last Meeting in Las Cruces
remembering Keith Wilson

                1.

I embrace your withered frame,
shocked how trauma and time
have wizened that image
I have carried of you.
Your body fragile as a child's,
eyes full of recognition,
tongue imprisoned.

                2.

Amigo, I recall the year
you drove me in your old VW van
from Las Cruces across the sands
to Alamagordo, over the Sacramentos
and east to Hobbs. You were
a most convincing travelogue
for New Mexico, the land you loved.
You fired my imagination
with history, lore and language.
It was the first time I heard
words like *caprock* and *llano estacado*
slip so easily off your tongue.
That was then.
You opened your world to me.

                3.

Now you are unable to utter
recognizable words. You can

no longer write at all, either
by the fountain pen you favored,
or by keyboard—you, who spent
a lifetime spinning tales,
seeding poems to bloom
like desert flowers after rain,
are now reduced to babble.

4.

O, but we spent so many
good hours together over food
and drink, talking poetry,
history, landscapes and friends,
long after wiser versions of ourselves
would have gone to bed.
There was a kinship, a bond
we both recognized.

Ever-present in your life,
your guardian spirit and wife,
constant companion,
now constant nurse.

5.

This last meeting is bittersweet.
Happiness is palpable in your face,
and though I fail to grasp
your attempts at words,
I can see and feel the joy
and I know your desire
to lend it words.

Since this will be
our last time together,
all I can do is give you
this gentle embrace,
this silent wish
for a safe journey.

November Hawks

I've often wondered where
the wintering grounds of prairie hawks
might be and now, between Hobbs and Artesia,
west of the caprock, my musing
meets the answer head-on.

Who'd have believed
this treeless *llano estacado,* fearsome plains,
would attract so many raptors?
Hawks of all sizes rest on anything
that places them above surrounding terrain —
fence posts, poles, corrals,
even large rocks in this treelessness
afford an essential perch.

These plains are not unlike my own,
so hawk-abundance should not surprise;
they, like me, have escaped the cold
where field mice sleep beneath snow
and the meals of summer are no more.
Under an open predatory sky we speed
towards Sacramento Mountain night.

Being Cast in Gallup

My friend says most New Mexicans
avoid Gallup whenever they can—its reputation,
especially its regard for Native Americans,
tarnished at best. But it's past lunchtime
and our appetites vote for a Gallup stop.
The young hostess, with a toss
of acrylic black hair, shrugs her shoulders,
loudly declares us as *seniors*
and totes up two discount lunches.

She has dealt us our parts and our script,
and so we hobble, stiff with miles of interstate,
deliberate and slow as judges,
around the buffet, our limbs lending
instant credibility to the unwanted roles
in which she has cast us. We pick
and choose our way around salads,
soups and hot entrees, thinking,
as we fork and spoon our plates full,
that the stage upon which we now play
will all too soon become permanent,
no masks, no acting required at all—
a fibrous thought to chew on
and swallow with our senior specials.

Mesa-top Lakes

We drive a gravel road
over miles of cattle and antelope range,
corkscrew slowly several hundred feet
up a twisty gouge of road to arrive
atop a large mesa—our destination:
the Charette Lakes,
unexpected trout waters perched
in the middle of a vast silence
where wind slides down
from Sangre de Cristo Mountains
to crack the dry husk of September.

In this hard-to-imagine location,
a twenty-first century wilderness,
two small lakes teem with trout,
surrounded by a lava rock plain
that hunches its rocky slopes
and drops them abruptly into the water.
On the level mesa bed of rock, sand
and gravel we set up camp.
Eavesdroppers around include chollas,
prickly pear cacti, octotillos,
clumps of yucca and a host of small plants
for which I have no name.

The Charettes seem an anomaly,
a misplacement. Yet they are here
and so are we, amazed they are here at all.
But not so much we can't unpack
our assorted angling gear and make
our way down over rocks
to the water's edge.

The Backyard World of Joe Somoza

Quite frankly, amigo, you amaze
hell out of me, even if hell is both
inept and inapt to describe scenes
you create in your backyard poems,

looking out your window on Hamiel
in Cruces, or sitting outside in your chair,
watching well fed cats creep or cavort,
or a spider scurry its way across a rock.

Amigo, you are one with this world
of the wondrously mundane of home.
Your language gift and your selfless
generosity share this with all of us.

This world is your own and you are
its living center; we can feel in each
moment chosen your beating heart.
We share your day with thanksgiving.

Pinons and Pine Nuts

Somewhere on the edge of Santa Fe we are parked
in an RV campground in the shade of pinons,
an arboreal feature of northern New Mexico.

Our site is strewn with fallen pinon clusters, husks
that hold the beginnings of new trees. The nuts
that have escaped the pods are everywhere and appear

versions of roasted coffee beans. Within the hull lies
the pinon seed or pine nut, favored in salads and baking,
once a staple of Ute and Paiute people.

A small woman with tiny dog moves among campsites,
scooping up clusters, squatting or bending in her foraging,
placing the sticky seeds into her plastic sack.

Later she will place them between sheets of cloth
or heavy plastic and, using a rolling pin, crack the hulls
to separate the outer husk from the aromatic seeds.

Gathering your own pine nuts will come at the cost
of an aching back and you will appreciate why pine nuts
in the supermarket will cost over ten dollars a pound.

If Place Names Mean Anything

then how fortunate
the New Mexico poet

who lives in a house
at the very foot

of Dragon Mountain
in Owl Canyon

After the Fall
remembering Henry D.

Intent on crossing the street, no cars in sight,
a man steps down from the street curb. This simple

act will change his life forever. He has crossed streets
here in his New Mexico hometown a thousand times.

An ordinary day, ordinary act. Why would this
day be different? He almost reaches the far curb

when one foot missteps, he trips, pitches head first
against the concrete curb, plunges into darkness.

Years later, he has zero memory of the moment,
the urgent ride by chopper to a medical center,

hours undergoing extensive brain surgery,
induced two-week coma, hovering neurosurgeons

studying him like an unexpected gift. He cannot
recall when he became this slow, shuffling old man.

Somewhere locked inside lie glimpses of a glib jokester,
a raconteur who once shared his now enfeebled body.

Does he believe he has always been this faltering speaker
who struggles to shape recognizable words into meaning?

Now that he has crossed safely that final darkness,
we who have streets to cross do so with measured care.

After the Poetry Reading in New Mexico

We are gathered at the home of a writer, relaxing after
the anxieties of performance, when the psycho arrives,
the same guy who sat at the back of the crowded bookstore
and fidgeted through the reading like a jock who'd left
the ball game to please his wife. He arrives at the party,
alone, pulls out a pocket flask, downs half,
then aims at me a rapid-fire critique of my reading,
which I do my level best to ignore.

Meanwhile, the man-with-many-hats sits across the room
practicing sleight-of-hat because he, too, seeks a spotlight.

But the psycho holds the floor, infused with bourbon
and a haphazard passion my poems appear to have loosed.
Some latent furies have seized him
and now his voice rises with a conviction
entirely unsupported by a modicum of sense.

Meanwhile, the man-with-many-hats passes them
from his hand to his head to hand to hat rack to hand
to head, the hats becoming a juggled blur.

The two of them finish together with a flourish
that even I can applaud.

Two Old Boys in a Half-ton

The day before Thanksgiving the highway thrums
with traffic as college students lug their laundry
and their fearsome appetites home for the three-day break,
a mega-stream of American youth that swells to a flood
as turkey and cranberries and sweet potatoes,
ham and creamed peas and lemon meringue pie
beckon family members from across the land
to the annual feast of plenty.

Between Safford and Silver City we spot
a stranded car—hood raised, two young women
poised before a stubborn Chevy. We stop,
offer assistance, poke our heads under the hood,
speculate about a faulty alternator,
finally offer the twosome a lift into Silver City.
We transfer their luggage and the college pair
crawl into the covered back of our half-ton.
It's not far, so the cramped ride will do little
to dampen their holiday spirits.

Rolling again, we reflect with some surprise
on the simple trust of this youthful pair,
who have climbed into the back of a half-ton
with two strangers who, for all they know,
could have less than noble motives.

We decide we must appear to them
just a pair of harmless old boys who pose
no threat; and we are shocked, perhaps
even disappointed—for this is not the way
we would have seen ourselves.
It is an unexpected kick in the groin;

and the two in the back who can't hear us
are no doubt laughing, swapping campus scandals,
oblivious to the ego-damage they've done.
After we've safely delivered the twosome
to their destination in Silver City, we journey on,
a bit subdued, nursing this unexpected wound,
wondering when it happened that we became
a pair of innocuous old codgers.

UNM Crows

The campus in Albuquerque is an oasis.
It dominates the landscape with greenery —
watered lawns, duck pond, flowers and fountain,
and leafy arms of trees, defiant against
the parched desert sky. Crows have made
the university campus winter home.

The President's wife of objects: this surfeit
of black-feathered migrants has darkened
her vision of Eden. She campaigns against them,
wants to force them further south — Las Cruces
would be an acceptable alternative to her.
She speaks of crow bounties, scare tactics,
to rid the campus of undesirable corvid migrants.

But the crows call in reinforcements: they home
in from all directions: corn-fed crows from
Nebraska and Kansas, pie-fed crows
from the fields of Minnesota, stoic crows
from the bleakness of North Dakota,
Even medicared crows down from Canada,
laconic crows from central Connecticut,
red-necked crows from Montana ranch lands,
radical crows from the mountains of Idaho,
windblown crows from the wilds of Wyoming,
Communist crows from the north end of Winnipeg,
New Age crows from northern New Mexico,
fundamentalist crows flown north from Texas,
slow-talking crows from Oklahoma.

UNM becomes part-academia, part-aviary:
crows on lawns and fences and benches,
crows on statues and walkways and stop signs,
crows on bushes and boxes and eaves troughs,
crows at bird baths and lamp posts and bus stops,
twenty thousand students, a hundred thousand crows.
The sky darkens as myriad numbers grow;
students and faculty cross the campus in groups,
casting frequent furtive glances overhead.

The Dancing Man of Santa Elena

Inside the cantina the dancing man
is on his feet, singing a Spanish song,
urging the little girl from her chair
to sing and dance with him.
She puts him to the test:
insists he don the straw sombrero
hanging on the wall. So he does
and she gets up beside him, attempts
to follow the movements of his feet,
as she sings the words with him.
The man is her grandfather's age
and she has never seen him
before this day in Santa Elena.

Outside an acetylene sun burns
the cloudless sky and whatever
is foolish enough to move.
Even dogs lie, tongues lolling,
under the few relic half-tons.
The only street of Santa Elena
still as an abandoned house.

But in the cantina the dancing man
and the little Mexican girl move
against heat and stillness,
move to the lilt of their voices—
dance through ages,
dance against time.

Fifty Thousand Coyotes Can't Be Wrong

Climbing up through the Organ Mountains
we pass through Cloudcroft—the name
conjures up sheep pastures. The weather is
cool but bright and a few small clouds
gambol over the New Mexico sky.

At Mayhill a neon Coors sign crooks a finger
from a small roadside saloon and I spin sharply
from the asphalt to stop before its door.
Mid-afternoon and Mayhill's so small we have
the place to ourselves, except for a few old boys
who stare at us without embarrassment
as we settle behind cans of Coors. Behind the bar
a fortyish man in a Miami Vice hat serves
and looks as if he wants to be elsewhere.
There's a WANTED sign behind him. It seems
what's wanted in Mayhill are good drinkers,
loose women and a piano player. In that order.

The sun is streaking the front window,
but the saloon is dark, until our eyes adjust
to the gloom and make out the small stage,
a pool table, a small adjoining card room,
and vacant tables ringed with vacant chairs.

The place could have been a set for "Gunsmoke,"
but it's near-empty and with lamb-clouds rollicking
through the sky, it's hard to imagine the joint alive
with leathery-faced cowpokes twisting smokes
from Bull Durham sacks, squinting at each other
through the smoke and dimness, while a fiddler
scrapes his bow and a guitarist beats out rhythm.

But fifty thousand coyotes can't be wrong,
another sign behind the bar assures.
It's urging us to eat more lamb, but lambs
are eating the light from the sky and we have
miles to drive before nightfall. Back in the car,
we wheel away from Mayhill, down to plains
that stretch to Texas and beyond. The lambs
have fled the sky and the coyote sun
shadows us all the way to Artesia.

Sea Dreams/War Dreams

I've been reading sea dreams
of a poet born in a desert landscape.
He took to sea, but the sea took
him to a warship off Korea.

Decorated a hero by his peers,
he returned to New Mexico
with shattered eardrum
and shattered illusions.
One impaired his hearing,
the other his view of humanity.

Though he took to the sea,
the sea took him, rolled him
under, only to bring him back
to surface at night at home
where ancient sea-beds were
his water by day,
his comfort by night.

The war his country asked
of him convinced him war
has no heroes. Only the dead.
That the cost of violence
is always more violence.
Sea, war, sand—all marked
him as one of their own.

Incident in Las Cruces

This is no cartoon roadrunner, self-assured and decisive.
We have driven 1200 miles of New Mexico without a sighting.

But here, stopped at a traffic light on Lohman Street
we see our first, darting back and forth, in a confusion

of cars and horns, caught where the unfamiliar intersects
with the strange, caught in the changing colours

of its own uncertainty. All traffic comes to a stop.
The lights keep changing as if there were no moment here

where for just a minute or two the motorized world stood still
to cheer its cartoon hero, until at last the befuddled bird

spots an opening and scurries away. Not a single coyote
among us to seek our moment of revenge.

Satisfaction Required

We've stopped at the bar in Mayhill without fail each time
we've passed this way and today the barmaid asks us for I.D.

Some joke! I'm a grandfather, many times over; my friend's
beard is snowy—that should say it all, no callow youths here.

Turns out the barmaid's serious, won't serve us beer until she
sees what she wants: a photo-graced driver's licence.

She says the new state law requires this procedure when
the server doesn't know by name or face her customer.

An old cowpoke on the next barstool says: *I been comin'
here forty years and she even made me go home for I.D.*

*They'll be shovellin me under before I ever show my I.D. again
for a goddam beer!* So now we have our beer and are satisfied;

the barmaid's satisfied that she's done her duty and can serve us;
the law's satisfied and even the old cowpoke looks near-happy.

IV. There Were Signs

Trouble in La Junta

The woman in the KOA office in this Colorado town wears
a name tag that announces: TROUBLE. That's enough to raise

any man's eyebrows, including mine. When I comment on it
she says, "I earned it—and more." Sounds like a story

I'm not sure I want to pursue, though the poet in me desires it.
A divorcee from San Diego, Trouble raises a school-aged son.

I ask about good eating spots in town and she wants to know
what kind of food. So I say Mexican and she informs me she is

very particular about Mexican food, coming from San Diego.
She is freckled and red-haired. "After all, I spent several years

as ... a *Lopez*," she adds, pausing, for additional illumination.
Troubled times loom in those words. She leans across the counter

and whispers in conspiratorial fashion, though we are the only
two people in the office, "I wouldn't touch any Mexican food here."

She recommends a restaurant a few miles down the road. I thank her
and turn towards the door. "No trouble at all," she says.

Whatever Happened to Jane Jayroe?

In Laverne, Oklahoma the people wait,
they await the return of their queen.

We drive beneath the banner on Main Street
proclaiming Laverne "Home of Jane Jayroe."
It intimates how she was showered
with kisses the day the crown was placed
upon her teary-eyed head as the new
Miss America of 1967.

The pride is still here in Laverne.
The banner must be newly done each year
as Lavernians relive that day.

But what of Jane Jayroe, where is she?
Whatever becomes of all the Jayroes?
Do they marry football heroes, grow fat,
become sippers of afternoon vodka,
have babies who will be football stars
or movie queens? Do they settle for
a few years of magazine covers,
before younger Miss Americas replace them?
Do they become talk show hosts or hookers?
Whatever happened to Jane Jayroe?
Did she abandon Laverne forever in 1967?

Jane Jayroe, wherever you are, come back.
Come home to Laverne, Oklahoma.
The banner shouts, folks grow restless.
The news is decades old. Crows' feet may

have lined your lovely face, Jane,
but in Laverne, Oklahoma it doesn't matter.
In Laverne the people wait, Jane.
They wait for you.

Easy Proof

The direct blame attributed
for an electrical outage

leaving over three thousand homes
without the least jolt of power

in and around Tishamingo,
somewhere in southern Oklahoma,

was laid at the incinerated feet
of a pole-climbing bobcat,

the remains of which were
smoldering atop the power pole.

No charges were laid.
No inquest will be held.

Mesa Verde

To think these ingenious Puebloans were building
apartment complexes beneath sandstone overhangs
long before Chaucer conceived his *Tales*,
long before Shakespeare penned a play,
before most great European Cathedrals poked
holes in scudding clouds, before Gutenberg
pressed words to paper; and a full millennium
before real estate developers and realty agents
with their lexicon of build, buy and sell.
It's hard *not to be impressed* at Mesa Verde.

It's also hard not to be impressed with people who
were able to cultivate and nurture grains atop a mesa
over 8,500 feet high in a land not known for rainfall,
then harvest those grains and cache them away
in their many-roomed communal dwellings to ensure
one year's bounty would offset another's failure.

Mind-boggling, too, that these marvels were built
without surveys or eco-studies, without blueprints
wrought by degreed architects. Yet look at these sites!
How can we not be impressed by how their buildings
meld so perfectly into the landscape that even today,
a thousand years later we are still discovering them
in remote canyons and out-of-the-way sites?
I have stood before them in amazement and awe.
If you have been there, you have done the same.

Narrow Gauge Railroad, Colorado

The Durango-Silverton locomotive huffs along
the close-set bands of steel following the Animas
River out of Durango. The year is 2004.

Fifty years before, I was freed from the bonds
of high school and set loose upon an unsuspecting world—
raw, uncouth and curious.

As cindery smoke trails back from the steam locomotive
and sets my eyes watering, coal fumes punch my memory:
I am eighteen and it is winter, before Christmas.

*I ride a mixed freight/passenger train from Compeer
to Kerrobert on the lone passenger coach, the train
carrying horses to Ontario, the only other rider,*

*the owner of the horses. It is stormy, bitterly cold.
The coach is heated by small coal heaters at either end
and we do our best to keep it livable by stoking each*

*in turn. Mid-coach is a parka zone, so we sit near one stove
or the other. The horseman disappears each time the train
stops to uncouple an empty or add a new freight car.*

*He goes somewhere up front to check on his horses
and I am left alone to shuttle from one stove to the other
in an energetic attempt to keep winter on the outside.*

All of this comes back, fueled by smoke and cinders,
with the pitch and yaw of this antique railway car,
snailing its way up the serpentine steel in Colorado,

where we look out a window at sheer rock wall
of Cascade Canyon on one side, or out and down
into tumbling waters of the Animas River far below.

Main Street in Scottsdale

Under a winter-blue desert sky my friend
rolls his half-ton Ford 150 into the first
empty parking space, wedged between

a glistening BMW and a sleek Lexus.
Up and down Main Street I see ours are
the only wheels worth less than 100 Gs.

It is only mid-morning and already Main
is resplendent with sun flashes off finishes
of luxury cars that have never seen mud.

Sun glints off gold and chrome strips,
ornaments of Jaguars, Porsches and Benzes:
the ultimate extravagance on radial tires.

Their drivers are now scouring galleries,
antique shops, boutiques and jewellery stores.
Credit cards whisper discreetly on counters.

We step out of the half-ton, peer down Main,
dazed as students given the wrong exam.
We clamber towards a plain cup of coffee.

They Said

      1.

A man who grew up in New York state
within sniffing distance of French's
mustard factory says:

> *You are what you spread*
> *on what you eat.*

      2.

The writer from New Mexico whose
favorite word is *earth* says:

> *I am not the desert*
> *but its name is not*
> *so far from mine.*

      3.

A woman in a Wyoming coffee shop
in a shrivelled town that once
rocked with 8,000 miners says:

> *Ain't no winds anywhere*
> *like Wyoming winds.*

      4.

A New Mexican who raised
fighting cocks and carved
walking sticks from desert sotol said:

> *Water don't clear until you*
> *get the hogs outta the crick.*

5.

A man in his sixties who
grew up on the Rio Grande
with a rifle in his hands says:

> *Each time I go out hunting*
> *I am young again.*

6.

An East Texas emcee who was
told to speak louder offered:

> *Y'all are just gonna*
> *have to listen louder.*

There Were Signs

In a small roadside diner
in Jeffrey City, Wyoming:

>THIS IS NOT
>BURGER KING
>YOU DON'T GET IT YOUR WAY
>YOU TAKE IT MY WAY OR
>YOU DON'T GET THE
>SON-OF-A-BITCH

In the only bar
in Mayhill, New Mexico:

>48% BITCH
>52% SWEETHEART
>DON'T PUSH IT!

Written in dust on the back of a bus
in Wickenburg, Arizona

>IT'S HARD TO MAKE A COMEBACK
>WHEN YOU HAVEN'T BEEN ANYWHERE

Sign in Bentley's House of Coffee & Tea, Tucson Arizona

>AT THE FEAST OF EGO
>EVERYONE LEAVES HUNGRY

V. Road Apples

La Junta, CO

In the RV campground,
on the FM jazz station
what we want to hear is Coltrane.

What we get instead
are coal trains, every fifteen minutes—
all the shuddering, black night long.

In southwestern Colorado range land

Enroute to Trinidad, at varying intervals
we spy a number of hand-lettered signs
posted at the corners of tracts of range land.

>   NOT FOR SALE
>   TO THE U.S. ARMY

Cattle ranchers do not appreciate competition
from the Pentagon for land in Colorado.

Trinidad, CO

In this historic mining town
at one foot of Raton Pass,
we go for a pasta feed
to Rino's Italian Ristorante.

Rino's is owned
by a music-loving family,
so family and even serving staff
take turns picking up the mike
and singing karaoke—
pop, country & western hits,
even classical Italian opera arias
from one of the singing family.

Wining and dining in Trinidad:
good food, good wine, good company.

Near Cimarron, NM

A bucket of stars. Music.
An up-country band from Denver
on an outdoor stage.
Campfires throw dancing light.
The drinks are cheap
and run downhill.
Saturday night in Cold Beer, New Mexico.

A most unlikely, nowhere place,
once called Colfax Tavern.
Not much ever happens,
but you better be here when it does.
Tonight, Halden Wofford and the Hi-Beams
sing "There's a Hippie in My House"
to wild applause.

Near Raton, NM

In Sugarite Canyon mule deer and wild turkeys
meander over and atop forgotten streets and paths,
crumbled foundations. An abandoned coal town.

High on a scenic look-out, we gaze across the canyon,
try to place ourselves into what-once-was.

Occasional glimpses of cement or standing brick—
all that remains of boom days when Sugarite miners
were an economy all to themselves, a dream of riches
being lived, even realized by some.

Consequences, NM

e through while banks crashed,
Washington anguished itself to a standstill,
world markets wobbled on the edge
of a financial abyss, American soldiers
were exploding in Iraq and Afghanistan
and the global economy burst like a cheap balloon.
Pension plans nose-dived. The world gasped.
Politicians booked new hair appointments.
Obama and McCain stumped the nation.

We never slowed or stopped in T or C.
We ignored it. Nor were we faced with
any moral dilemma in doing so,
nor prompted to a single decision.

What consequences
in such an absence of truth?

Nutt, NM

It is so utterly insignificant
there isn't even a horse
around to qualify it
as a one-horse town.
But it does have a bar
that proclaims
the middle of nowhere—
a rarity in our times:
honest advertising.

Silver City, NM

At Lotta Gelatto
I ask the owner whether
he makes his own gelatto.

His face screws itself into
a picture of utter dismay.
"Any idiot can *sell* gelatto.
But only a few can make it."

Deming, NM

Embolism from Alabama
and Aneurysm from Michigan camp
in the site adjacent to us in the RV park.
They are both recuperating from surgery.

Embolism has had her skull surgically
sundered and is just regaining speech,
she tells me, her words delivered
one difficult birth after another.

Aneurysm has had his chest cleaved,
a quadruple bypass, a stroke thrown
into the mix for good measure; he is
now relearning the use of his limbs.

Here in Deming, they both hope
their shiny new RV with all its perks,
with the change of scenery and climate,
will help them adjust to new versions
of the person each married long ago.

The City of Rocks State Park, NM

north of Deming has camp sites,
but we are warned about
aggressive bees
and about rattlesnakes,
aggressive or not.
The visitor center
displays names and describes
many resident species
of unfriendly vipers.

A sun-bleached desert crone
in the visitor center
assures us rattlesnakes,
once reported, are quickly captured
by park wardens
and transported
miles away for release.

How many hours
would it take one such
apprehended rattlesnake
to undulate its way back
to its mate and to what
it might consider home?

Silver City, NM

Colette is our waitress in Dianne's Restaurant,
her name tag informs us. I point out the window
across the street at a tree with what
looks like crinkly yellow fruit hanging
from lower branches and I ask,
"What is that tree and fruit called?"

Colette stares past gauzy curtains,
steadies her gaze a few seconds
before turning to me and saying:
"I have no idea. I've never even
noticed those things before."

Her words say something about
both of us. We both remain ignorant—
on one subject at least, and for now.

Just east of Hobbs, NM

we cross the state line and roll onto west Texas
flatlands known for cotton, oil wells and the Bushes.
I am advised by road sign:

    DRIVE FRIENDLY

Within a half-hour, we encounter a semi hauling
what seems a partial missile shell on a flatbed trailer.
It goes by at high speed. I see no identification on it.

We reach Amarillo and find an RV park. As I check in
at the office I notice a .45 revolver mounted on the wall
and a sign below that reads: WE DON'T DIAL 911.

Seminole to Amarillo

We roll across landscape so horizontal
you think the land a perfect line
shouldering the sky. Overhead,
brilliant unmarked blue.

On this hill-less hardscrabble plain,
fields of cotton whisper in the wind
to fields of sorghum or peanuts,
earthy messages interrupted only by
bovine assertions from nearby range
where ranchers assert historic claim.

Every so often, a pecan grove interjects
an exclamation point in all this crop
and cattle declaration, seeming as much
out of place here as tumbling cascades,
or booming surf on this treeless tabletop.

Amarillo, TX

There surely must be a government regulation,
at the very least an axiom of common practice,
that accounts for the reason an RV park
or campground *must,* by definition it seems,
be located adjacent to a busy railroad line.

Palo Duro Canyon Park, TX

was once part of Charlie Goodnight's
vast cattle empire. Goodnight herded
thousands of longhorns, beginning
in the 19th century, bawling
their dusty way into the 20th
through generations of Goodnights.

When you look down into the yawning
sandstone chasm, it seems inconceivable
anyone should have amassed a fortune here.

Imagine yourself a lone cow hand
riding that walled canyon below,
feeling like a miner below ground
counting down hours and days
until you could ride out of darkness
to see and feel the sun again.

Groom, TX

On I-40 we can see it rise
above the distant skyline
long before we spot the town.

A humungous cross,
an affront to anyone
who appreciates subtlety
or understatement, especially
in matters of religious belief.

East of Amarillo

we come to a blip on the road map
that proclaims itself
birthplace of Roger Miller.

Well, dang me!

Near Alfalfa, OK

Acres and acres of reds
                    and golds,
an amazing burst
                    of sudden acrylic flash
in an uninspired,
                    drab landscape.

Canna lilies,
                    a vast field of them,
their blooms
now nearly spent,
                    but still
vibrant enough
                    to counterpoint
the cloudless autumn sky.

Norman, Oklahoma

We are walking towards
the Sooners' University,
on our morning fitness ritual,
far from alone in our strides,
though we may be
the oldest walkers here.

I am thinking,
they must allow children
to attend university these days:

they are all
so unforgivably young.
And beautiful!

Ah, but then,
so were we,
once...
so were we.

North of Oklahoma City, along I-35

It appears Johnny Appleseed
erupted into a manic phase here:
apple trees in wind-breaks,
or scattered at random,
some loaded with yellow fruit.

So much fruit and no pickers?
Fruit trees seem incongruous
in all this cattle range and farm land.
Strange, we say to ourselves.
Are there no nibbling deer,
no nocturnal apple-eaters?

Guthrie, OK

North of Oklahoma City we stop
for lunch in the Victorian Tea Room.
Downtown Guthrie is a splendid preservation
of late 19th and early 20th century storefronts,
replete with cupolas and gargoyles,
a bizarre hybrid of England
and the American frontier.

We sip Earl Grey tea direct from
Jolly Olde England via Connecticut.
No crumpets or scones for me.
I have piquant Southwest chili,
jalapeño cornbread.

Guthrie again. Walgreens

The young man on duty
in the camera department
has hair only Lyle Lovett
could truly appreciate.
His hairdo would drive
Pit Bulls into hiding.

Somewhere in Guthrie
lives an agitated mom
who daily shakes her
husband's family tree,
hoping something might
fall to earth
that could possibly
explain her son.

CPSIA information can be obtained at www.ICGtesting.com
Printed in the USA
BVOW02s0259010615

402645BV00003B/126/P